SOUL SISTERS

SOUL SISTERS

Women in Scripture
Speak to Women Today

EDWINA GATELEY

With Art by
LOUIS GLANZMAN

ORBIS BOOKS

Maryknoll, New York 10545

Fourth printing, July 2003

Founded in 1970, Orbis Books endeavors to publish works that enlighten the mind, nourish the spirit, and challenge the conscience. The publishing arm of the Maryknoll Fathers & Brothers, Orbis seeks to explore the global dimensions of the Christian faith and mission, to invite dialogue with diverse cultures and religious traditions, and to serve the cause of reconciliation and peace. The books published reflect the views of their authors and do not represent the official position of the Maryknoll Society. To learn more about Maryknoll and Orbis Books, please visit our website at www.maryknoll.org.

Library of Congress Cataloging-in-Publication Data

Gateley, Edwina.
    Soul sisters : women in Scripture speak to women today / Edwina
Gateley ; with art by Louis Glanzman.
        p. cm.
    ISBN 1-57075-443-8 (pbk.)
    1. Women in the Bible—Meditations. 2. Bible. N.T.
Gospels—Meditations. I. Title.
BS2445 .G33 2002
225.9'22'082—dc21
                                        2002004829

For Carolyn
My Soul Sister

Contents

Preface

When I first saw prints from Louis Glanzman's paintings of twelve of the women of the New Testament, something happened inside me. It was as if I suddenly recognized beloved sisters whom I had never seen before but knew in my heart. The paintings had a life of their own—unique, powerful, and as real as any living woman. They rose from the prints and spoke to me. After a lifetime of knowing *all about* the women of the Gospels, I felt that at last I had actually met them. Indeed I had. They were women whom I had encountered and connected with in my own life. They were homemakers, sex workers, child runaways, crones, teachers, mothers, senior citizens—and all of them knew Jesus. All of them were archetypes who reflected the journeys, struggles, joys, and dreams of women today.

I confess, with some humility, that I was somewhat surprised that a male artist could have so accurately and compassionately captured the personalities and feelings of these women in the Gospels—until, that is, I read more about Louis Glanzman and came to realize his awesome artistic credentials and talent. Among many other accomplishments,

Glanzman has painted some of the most memorable covers for *Time* magazine (more than eighty), the *New Yorker,* the *Saturday Evening Post,* and many other publications. He has illustrated numerous children's books, including the classic Pippi Longstocking series. His works occupy prominent space in public and private art collections throughout the United States and in Europe. His prolific illustrations, portraits, and historical paintings have won him acclaim as one of America's great artists. But for me Louis Glanzman was also the only man I knew who had met and understood the women in the Gospels on such a deep, intuitive level.

Glanzman was the catalyst for a personal spiritual experience which I knew had forever deepened my love and soul connection with the women he had painted. He had captured their souls in art. Driven by the power of this experience, I did something unprecedented. I called Orbis Books (whom I had learned were going to publish the paintings) pleading—and practically demanding—that they choose me as the poet/author for the book! The publisher, Mike Leach, who was already putting together a short list of potential authors (among whom I was not yet included!), was clearly impressed with my passion and conviction! "These are my soul sisters," I pleaded. "I know their stories and they can only be told in poetry—for they belong to us all." In retrospect I am somewhat awed by my audacity. But it worked! The next day Mike called. I was to be the poet for Louis Glanzman's paintings—an awesome and sacred task that left me not a little apprehensive in spite of my conviction.

The writing of *Soul Sisters* became as much a spiritual experience as a work of poetry. As I spent time with each woman, I knew a deepening understanding of who she was and what she had experienced. Entering into her story of two thousand years ago, I tried to capture it in poetry and in so doing realized that I was also writing the stories of women I know today. The journey and its stories belong to us all. I knew that others, both men and women, would be blessed as I was, to connect on a deeper level with the women around Jesus—our Soul Sisters.

EDWINA GATELEY
MAY 2002

Elizabeth

When Elizabeth's time for delivery arrived, she gave birth to a son. Her neighbors and relatives, upon hearing that the Lord had extended his mercy to her, rejoiced with her. When they assembled for the circumcision of the child on the eighth day, they intended to name him after his father Zechariah. At this time his mother intervened, saying, "No, he is to be called John."

Luke 1:57-60

Elizabeth! Elizabeth!
How did you survive
so many years
bowed down by humiliation?

The meaning and purpose
of your womanhood
defined so absolutely
by your culture.
You were born,
they declared,
to give birth—
the only accepted purpose
for woman—
for marriage—
for your existence—
to give birth
to another.
But what of you, Elizabeth?
What of your life
    your dreams
    your hopes
    your gifts
    your hidden tears?
What, Elizabeth, of your voice?
It was not heard
nor counted
against the rise and swell
of male voices
defining and ruling your world.

How did it feel, Elizabeth,

to hear,

beneath the ringing voices,

the whispers of the women—

your sisters—

trapped too

in a system

encircling them in iron boundaries

of appropriate behavior?

Did you sense their pity

as they glanced your way—

veiled eyes measuring

the betraying flatness

of your belly?

Did you hear

their murmurs

of disapproval,

at your failure to perform

as a woman—

thus failing and betraying

all of womankind?

Did you flinch, Elizabeth,

before your husband's eyes—

bearing down upon you

in bitter disappointment

and public humiliation?

Did you feel a Defect, Elizabeth?
(For that, indeed,
was how you were regarded
in your partiarchal culture.)
But not you, alone, sister,
for things have not changed
that much
since you burned with shame.
Women, worldwide,
are still deemed
essentially
birthers of others,
not birthers of themselves.
Throughout our globe
woman is still
invisible—
counted as little with child
and as nothing without.
Your desperate prayers
for justification
of your womanhood
are joined, Elizabeth,
by millions of your sisters
still to this very day.
But, where once you whispered prayers

to prove your worth

through pregnancy,

now women's voices rise

a little louder

to claim their own dignity

just as they are—

standing defiant

on their own two feet

against the definition

of history.

Were you

to put your ear

to the earth, Elizabeth,

you would feel the swell

of women's voices,

pulsing in energy,

rising from the dust

and clay of Africa,

the mountains of the East,

the forests and plains

of the Americas,

the cities of Europe,

and the frozen plains

of the north.

The whole globe, Elizabeth,

now shakes with the voices

of your sisters,

no longer whispering,

their spirits no longer

curled up in shame—

fetus-like—

but with arms

stretched around

the Universe—

reaching to touch and comfort

their sisters

in Turkey,

Northern Ireland,

Afghanistan,

Mexico,

Thailand,

Rwanda and

the United States of America

where women are still locked up

and damned forever

for the tragic consequences

of Postpartum Depression

which our men

can never, never know

nor understand.

There is much indeed,

we do not yet understand

about womanhood

and motherhood.

But one thing is sure, Elizabeth,

we ourselves,

women themselves,

must determine who we are.

That time was not

for you.

God alone

intervened for you, Elizabeth,

in secret, silent,

redemptive act

you didn't even know about.

You only waited

> dreaming

> hoping

> longing

> loving—

as women do.

And the miracle came about—

seeding where none could see.

Right in the heart

of the system,

you denied them

their condemnation.

Woman—

you rose and swelled

in spite of the improbability,

the impossibility!

And you left them,

aghast and babbling

at the rising

of your belly.

For you were old, Elizabeth—

no longer smooth-skinned

and slim and dark—

but wrinkled and thickening

and silvering.

Now you were a crone—

having passed through youth,

maidenhood

and maturity

into the darkness of women's secrets

where we see and understand things

from a deep place of dying

and letting go.

It was there,

in the womb of the crone,

that Wisdom made her home.

And only you, Elizabeth,

knew Her rising and collusion!

Sophia Wisdom—

elusive spirit

of a Mother God—

shifting, stirring, seeding

in place

that none could see!

Then Mary,

young, vibrant

and also filled

with new life,

hurried to your home,

to share Good News,

to embrace and hold—

as women do their sisters.

Did she know that you

the crone,

the older woman,

was pregnant too?

Was her visit,

so far from home,

a casual trip?

Or did she follow

her woman instinct—

obey a dream—

intuit an event—

listen to the inner wisdom

which drove her

to connect with you,

wise crone?

You came together,

as women do,

to celebrate

the new life

enmeshed in moist womb.

Mothers of Salvation!

Mary stayed with you,

waiting for fullness of time,

as women do,

comforting and holding,

encouraging the birthing

against all odds.

Until your child—

yet another miracle

from a woman's womb,

was born.

And through it all,

the man Zechariah,

remained silent—

struck dumb before the wonder,

his task only

to watch,

spectator of the miracle.

But now it was you, Elizabeth,

who spoke aloud

before your husband's dumbness—

declaring the name of your son:

He is John.

Sweeping aside custom and convention,

dismissing the protests

of relatives and friends,

You, who had heard the voice of God

in silence—

now spoke it aloud.

And no one, Elizabeth,

dared rebuke you,

Soul Sister.

Anna the Prophetess

There was also a certain prophetess, Anna by name, daughter of Phanuel of the tribe of Asher. She had seen many days, having lived seven years with her husband after her marriage and then as a widow until she was eighty-four. She was constantly in the temple, worshiping day and night in fasting and prayer. Coming on the scene at this moment, she gave thanks to God and talked about the child to all who looked forward to the deliverance of Jerusalem.

Luke 2:36-38

Anna, prophetess of God!
the little we know of you
reveals a woman of awesome wisdom
whose intuition and inner sight
knew what was to come.

Your prophetic gift
lives with us still, Anna—
gestating deep
in our feminine consciousness.
Your words
still waiting to be uttered
in our time.
You were, Anna,
a daughter of Ancient Tradition
that embraced a Mother God
and never questioned
the sacred role of women
in prophecy, discernment and
moral leadership.
For, in ancient times,
women were honored
as the embodiment of wisdom,
reflecting in the cycles
of their lives
the wonder of creation
and intrinsically connected
to the divine
through the mysterious powers of birthing.
But when you had passed through
the first two cycles of womanhood—
Maiden and Mother—
you then entered into
the dark age of the Crone, Anna—
The Old One,

wrinkled,
wise,
known from time immemorial as
The Saga—
"She Who Speaks,"
the one who now,
in her old age,
had reached the fullness of her time
and was empowered by her years
to utter sacred words and poetry,
invoking the divine
in the Temple's holy spaces.
Oracle of the Sacred!
The Book of Proverbs
knew you, Anna:
"She opens her mouth with wisdom"
    (Prov. 31:26).
And the people of your time
knew you too—
more connected than we
to the wisdom of the feminine
and the power of the Crone—
they honored your wrinkles
as a sign of knowledge and experience
to be shared as a gift
with those who had not walked
so far and deeply,
and were unfamiliar
with the mysteries of life and death.

They called you "Hag"—
meaning in those early days
not one to be despised and cast aside,
but a wise and holy woman.
Priestess and Prophetess,
Counselor and Guide,
you were a comfort and a solace
to God's people, Anna!
Ah, wise woman!
We have lost you!
We are disconnected
from the feminine power and energy
that breathed through your wrinkled,
   craggy skin.
We are all too often
bereft
of the compassion,
born of long journeying,
that shone through
your all-seeing eyes.
But, above all,
We fear you, Anna, Prophetess!
We flee your cracks and wrinkles,
your silver hair and
fragile bones.
We fear all the signs of age
that set you
in a place of honor—
beloved by all.

Now in our time
they have become
signs of shame and humiliation.
Our world supplies us, Anna,
with a vast array
of creams and colors and lotions,
pills and masks and potions
to hide and change
the image of the Crone!
To smooth out,
> wipe away

> cut out

> tuck away

those very signs
which proclaimed you
honored and holy!
Our menfolk
don't like it, Anna.
They want us Maiden.
or Mother.
Not Crone.
They want us—demand us—
cute, pretty, safe or comforting.
The Crone is none of those things.
She stands apart
in a darker place,
a deeper place
where we do not wish to go . . .
She challenges

our false imaginings
and our flight
from wisdom and dying.
We are so afraid of dark, old places.
We do not want to be there.
It is not a popular place to be.
We will do anything
to hold back the knowing.
We have made
the cloak of the Crone
so unacceptable.
So ugly.
So we do not want to know
the mysteries it would hide.
We retreat
from the feminine insights
of your years, Anna!—
lest our lives and our world
be changed forever.
For if we embrace you, Crone,
Wisdom figure,
Ancient Female lodged so deep
in our psyches
stirring like an embryonic volcano
in our collective human consciousness—
We, your sisters,
silent so long,
will also prophesy and
utter sacred songs and canticles!

And our prophecy
will claim the honor
in which age
and all life
must be held.
We will speak aloud
of things hidden
and denied
and not recognized.
We, your sisters,
will proclaim as you did Anna,
that God is in our midst—
not in power and triumph,
control and hierarchy,
but in the small,
  the humble
  the un-acknowledged.
Your wisdom, Anna,
revealed to you
the deeper truths
from which we hide
when we deny
the beauty and significance of age.
Anna, sister, prophetess,
Speaker of the truth,
help us reclaim
that which we have left behind—
our woman gifts—abandoned,
our journey aborted and denied

in our sad efforts

to hide

from all that we could be.

May we, Anna,

Women of today,

inheritors of a world unbalanced,

bereft of feminine wisdom,

and grieving

while not even knowing

what we grieve,

may we retrieve

the Crone, the Wise Woman,

the Prophetess

from the layers of our history.

May we once again delight

in access

to sacred mysteries—

waiting and given

to those who honor their years,

listen to their lives, reflect on their experience,

embrace who they are,

discern their sacred path

and dare follow it—

distilling

all they have encountered

and experienced on their way

into a chalice of Wisdom

for others to taste.

May we, Anna, prophetess,
stand up with courage,
breaking open
our own truth,
like you,
in the Temple's sacred spaces.
Soul Sister.

Mary

. . . The Virgin's name was Mary. Upon arriving, the angel said to her: "Rejoice, O highly favored daughter! The Lord is with you. Blessed are you among women." She was deeply troubled by his words, and wondered what his greeting meant. The angel went on to say to her: "Do not fear, Mary. You have found favor with God. You shall conceive and bear a son and give him the name of Jesus . . . "

Luke 1:27-33

"Do not be afraid . . ."
The words made no sense
in your reality, Mary—
terrified, pregnant teen
creeping around in a land occupied
by men of the sword.

Is that what you thought, Mary?—
Child runaway,
desperate for a hiding place
to release
your fear and confusion?
Do not be afraid.
That's what Elizabeth would say too.
You knew it.
Your female instinct told you
she would hold you, guard you
from prying eyes and gossip.
And so you hurried, Mary,
as runaways do,
following a long journey
to seek the comfort
of an older woman.
You did not even need to speak, Mary,
for Elizabeth knew
(as women do)
that you carried a child within you.
She recognized the signs
of pregnancy,
and her heart
leapt with joy for you, Mary!
Do not be afraid,
she murmured—
It is a blessing!
How she must have held you!
Smiled upon you,

soothed away your fears
with tender caress
of work-worn hands.
And then you knew, Mary,
that you were not alone.
You were connected,
in a mysterious, powerful way,
with every woman
who ever gave birth in human history.
Blessed Mary! Blessed are you!
Bearer of hope for the world!
Co-creator—
graced by divine mystery
to mother-love
swelling your belly with redemption!
Ah, Mary!
How your soul sang
with fullness and gratitude—
awed and raised up
by the miracle of mothering
given to women
and given, now, to you—
the small, the insignificant,
the one without a man
whom God raised up,
lavishing in blessing!

Affirmed, loved and comforted,
you stayed with Elizabeth—

to safely nurture
your fragile dream.
Like so many other women
who flee violence,
clutching their babies,
you crossed the border defining you
a stranger,
dependent on foreign aid, welfare
and hand-outs—
the charity of others—
to feed the Son of God.
But the words,
Do not be afraid,
never left you in that time of loss!
Drawing on the wisdom and courage
Elizabeth had shared with you,
you grew into motherhood.
Like a lioness
protecting and feeding her young
with ferocious devotion,
you harbored and nurtured the life
which would forever change
world history:
Prince of Peace.
Light to all Nations.
Ah, Mary!
Uprooted and displaced,
you held on to your visions and dreams
in a foreign land.

You remembered the light
you had once seen
and the words you once had heard
stirring in your soul, calling you
to an untrod path
lit only by a star.
Mary, fugitive,
Did you also feel,
wrapped around you in a foreign land,
Elizabeth's warm embrace?
Did you at night,
when you were lonely and afraid,
remember her gentle friendship?
Did it stay with you—
like a warm blanket—
until at last,
You could return to your own land and home?
And as you gathered your things
to start all over again,
did you long, Mary,
as we all do,
for a peaceful, normal life—
a nice domestic routine
with regular meals—
and grandchildren?
Slowly,
then it seemed so rapidly,
You watched your child grow—
Wondering how he would be

leaving their mothers
grieving in secret,
stroking and kissing
abandoned playthings.
And so you watched and waited,
wept and prayed,
Letting go
slowly and reluctantly,
as mothers must,
of all claims and expectations . . .
Leaving you, Mary,
All emptied out—
Bereft now
of son,
and grandchildren—
Stolen away
by the realm of God.
Only the Word
was left for you,
Mary,
Mother of the Afflicted.
And even that
was wrenched from you
when they killed him.
Only silence.
Dark silence
was left you,
Mary, Mother of Sorrows,

And a grief
Too deep to imagine,
Etching in your soul
deep spaces
for Wisdom
to make Her home.
Your journey
has blessed ours, Mary.
Your Yes dares us
to believe in the impossible,
to embrace the unknown,
and to expect the breaking through of mystery
onto our bleak and level horizons.
The words you heard, Mary,
We will forever remember.
We will not be afraid,
for the life that you birthed
will not be extinguished
in our souls.
And the journey
you took in faithfulness,
we also take.
We the women, the midwives,
and the healers will also,
like you Mary, soul sister,
Give birth to God
for our world.

he Widow's Mite

He glanced up and saw the rich putting their offerings into the treasury, and also a poor widow putting in two copper coins. At that he said: "I assure you, this poor widow has put more than all the rest. They make contributions out of their surplus, but she from her want has given what she could not afford—every penny she has to live on."

Luke 21:1-4

What must it really be like
to have nothing?
What must it really be like
not to know
whether you will eat tomorrow?
Stark poverty

is really quite a nasty thing—
it has an odor
all of its own
which seeps through
broken skin
and threadbare clothing—
hiding in the crumpled crevices
drawn tight against the cold.
Poverty is uncomfortable,
not only for those who live with it,
but also and perhaps, especially,
for those who merely observe.
For are we not all,
as they say,
a paycheck or two from poverty?
Are we not all susceptible
to sudden and unexpected tragedy
that could cast us,
pitilessly,
into that grey and insubstantial place
where dignity and self-respect
stand hostage to hand-outs?
What must it feel like
to line up for benefits—
hands outstretched, like a baby's,
to catch the crumbs that fall
from corporate table?
I do not know.

I pray I never will.
I can only speculate and imagine,
watch and wonder . . .
Perhaps even . . . perhaps,
I can break open my heart enough
to let the mystery in, to risk empathy
with this other woman
standing there
    on the street corner,
    outside the shelter,
    the soup kitchen,
    the church,
clutching her pennies
like gold.
Just for a moment—
a short, cringing moment—
I could be her . . .
And, in a second of redemption,
I am.
Fingering the two pennies
hiding deep in my pocket,
I stare at the collection box
rising, intrusive, daring,
before me,
jangling
"World Hunger!"
in coppery dance.
Empathy evaporates

at the enormity of the demand.
Redemption retreats.
I am no longer
the other woman,
the one with the two copper coins,
for I know in all of my being,
that I would never—
could never—
let go my two coins,
no matter how small they are . . .
They are all I have.
That's reasonable.
Reasonable too,
to let go the speculation and
imagined empathy.
Better not pretend
to understand
how she could even
unclench her fist
and drop her coins
into the hands of another.
But she did.
I am not her.
We are separate.
Different.
I am small spectator of something
bigger than me . . .
Is she there simply to leave me
gaping,

my claimed worthiness
resentfully unraveling
before her goodness?
I wish she had not intruded
into my heart,
quickening its beat.
But I must look again, sister,
impelled by your eyes—
brighter
than the glinting coins,
moist with incipient tears,
shining and reflecting
a wisdom
born of anguish.
Poverty did not suck dry
the richness of your spirit, sister!
It could not squeeze small
your generous heart,
but left you rich
in wisdom.
Your eyes
tell your story, sister,
and I must listen—
locked in your honest gaze.
For you have captured me,
and your deep-welled goodness
softens and reminds me of,
my essential self—
before I sold my soul

to Security and Comfort
and Compromise.
I think I love you.
And I tremble
in that truth—
for I looked into your eyes
and I cannot, ever,
be the same.
You have given more,
Jesus said,
than all the rest . . .
You have given more
than I . . .
For I have never been
that poor,
I have never been
that rich.
There was another woman,
you remind me of:
Her eyes were deep,
like yours.
She, too, was old and poor,
skin all dried and wrinkled.
I met her
when I was a young woman—
a missionary in Africa.
It was a troubled time.
Tribal warfare was strangling

a once lovely, fertile country.
Hunger and fear eclipsed the land
leaving its people trembling.
Most white folks left—
(wealth and privilege equal choice).
But some of us stayed
in solidarity
with the people
we had come to serve.
It was hard, though.
We couldn't travel
to shop for food and stuff.
So we didn't have much.
But we knew that the local folks
had a lot less than us—
they always did—
But even more so now . . .
One day as I stood outside my little house,
I saw an old woman
shuffling towards me,
clutching a package
all wrapped tight in banana leaves.
She looked up at me—
bent as she was and badly stooped—
But her eyes were deep and moist,
like yours, sister.
She had no coins,
just the banana parcel

which she thrust into my hands.
Her words stay with me still:
"Thank you for staying with us"
whispered in broken English.
Then off she stumbled,
anonymous,
back into the bushes
from where she had crept.
Intrigued,
I peeled away the banana leaves,
and found there,
all snuggled and warm together,
the gift,
the treasure—
three tiny chicken eggs . . .
All she had,
given to me,
though I had all.
Three tiny eggs—
a fortune
against her poverty,
the Widow's Mite—
for me.
What are we to say or do
before such goodness?
What is the gift
to do to me—
given my million mites?

How can I ever
personify
the generosity
in that little gift—
daring me to greatness?
How dare you, Jesus,
with your penetrating vision,
your discomfiting words,
leave me struggling in such a space!
How dare you, African woman,
leave me your three precious eggs—
weighing me down
with your treasures!
I can neither abandon
nor forget them.
Your eggs,
like the coins your sister gave,
are eternally held within me.
But, even more profoundly,
locked in my deepest knowing,
are your eyes, sister,
like burning lights calling me
to divest and share
my bounty—
my eggs—
to trade my accumulated goodies
for a richer spirit
transparent in simplicity,

lovely in nakedness—
but, oh, so vulnerable!
Dare I, sister,
trade my treasures
for grace-soaked soul?
Or are my treasures found,
not so much in the coins themselves,
as in the desire to hold them?
And are the riches
that I must share,
graces of the spirit
rather than goods of the earth?
Far more precious than silver or gold
or stocks and shares . . .
Dare I dig into my heart
to bring forth kindness,
tolerance and love
beyond expectation,
beyond reason,
to flow like a river
all around me,
soothing and refreshing
dry and lonely spaces
kept hidden in human souls?
Ah, is that it?
Must I become as God—
all emptying,
all compassion,

cracking open my heart
to pour out who I am.
Is that it?
Is that it? Soul sister,
will I be you?
Soul Sister.

$\mathcal{M}$artha

On their journey Jesus entered a village where a woman named Martha welcomed him to her home. She had a sister named Mary, who seated herself at the Lord's feet and listened to his words. Martha, who was busy with all the details of hospitality, came to him and said, "Lord, are you not concerned that my sister has left me to do the household tasks alone? Tell her to help me." The Lord in reply said to her: "Martha, Martha, you are anxious and upset about many things; one thing only is required. Mary has chosen the better portion and she shall not be deprived of it."

Luke 10:38-42

Ah, Martha, Martha!
The centuries have defined you
and dismissed you.
For you did not sit,

silent and submissive,
at the feet of Jesus, as Mary did.
No—you went about your business
of sifting and kneading and baking bread
to break open and feed the hungry.
You shook the cloth,
lined up the dishes,
placed the mats,
and prepared the table
for all to eat.
You were like my friend Sally,
who every day
stands over hot stoves
in steamy kitchen,
stirring soups and stews,
and brewing jugs of chocolate
to feed the hungry kids,
who just keep on coming and coming,
with empty bellies
from crumbling tenement homes,
sniffing out the warmth
and promise of nourishment
drifting in great clouds of goodness
from her kitchen.
You, like Sally, got on
with feeding the hungry, Martha.
And you did not hesitate to speak aloud—
demanding due assistance—
when women were expected to be silent.
Disapproval fell heavily upon you, Martha,

when you stepped out of place
in the name of service.
The words of reproof
were bitter
to your womanly pride,
a snub on your gift of baking:
Sitting and listening is better . . .
Better than . . . Better than the role of mother,
caregiver . . . baker?
Better than the work
of one who welcomes
and offers hospitality?
Did you cringe with humiliation, Martha?
Did your warm, giving, aproned body
tighten in shame?
What were you to do, Martha,
with the empty bellies?
What were you to do
with warm, baked bread
waiting to be broken?
Ah, Martha—
I think you did everything
you had to do,
Everything you had always done
when no one else was there—
     to bake,
     to wash,
     to serve,
     to feed.
You kept on doing it, Martha—

the work that was essential
and despised.
You knew you had to—
there simply was
no alternative . . .
But there, deep within,
where no one saw,
you wrestled with your wonderings,
fighting tears and biting your lips
to defy those insistent misgivings,
whispering your failures,
your lack of fulfillment,
your poor choice of career—
when, really, there was no choice . . .
Your life's work
necessary, but unsacralized.
Oh, did you wish, Martha,
that there was no bread
and no table?
Did you dream, too,
of just sitting and receiving,
instead of giving
      giving
      giving?
But that is what you did.
And that is what we do, soul sister . . .
Generation after generation,
we women have prepared the meal,
    waited at the table,
    cleaned the house,

done the dishes . . .
and dreamed
of sitting—
just like Mary did.
But we live with our reality,
we women know it well,
as you did.
There is work to be done.
> Bread to be baked.
> Clothes to be washed.
> Children to be fed.
And we must get on with it
as you did
and simply dream of lazier times.
Mature and responsible,
you knew what had to be done, Martha.
You did it,
but you also let it be known—
no pushover you,
you voiced your protest
in the midst of a culture
that preferred and acknowledged
submissive, silent women.
Standing defiant and strong,
you stood also for all of us who,
throughout the ages,
have given our lives in love and service,
yet often longed,
in quiet moment,
as the last crumbs were wiped away

and the last dish stored,
for a little recognition,
a touch of respect,
for the caregiver's awesome task.
Stubborn, passionate Martha!
You knew what was required,
no matter what was said.
You spoke your own
experienced truth.
You challenged dismissive definitions
of the woman's role,
and pushed beyond them,
daring to confront Jesus
(yet again!)
by the tomb
of your beloved brother—Lazarus.
While Mary cried at home
lost in grief,
You took charge of yours,
and challenged Jesus,
reminding him of who he was,
pushing the boundaries of his possibilities,
naming his divine authority—
the power of Life over Death . . .
"Even now I know
that anything you ask,
God will give to you.
For you are the Christ,
the Son of the living God."
Now DO IT!

Do what you have to do!
Stubborn, demanding Martha!
Expectant of the impossible—
knowing what must be done
and demanding accountability—
Get on with it!
And Jesus did.
At the word of the woman—
Pragmatic, no-nonsense,
life is short—
Jesus called forth Lazarus . . .
While Mary wept,
You, Martha,
as usual,
were about the business of life—
the business of the body—
demanding,
in your rousing style,
a resurrection.
And, caring so deeply,
involved so totally,
enmeshed so emotionally
in this business of life—
you elicited that resurrection!
No limitations here,
caregiver woman!
No small part to play here,
home-maker!—
Challenger of Jesus,
Namer of the Messiah,

Mistress of the home,
Wise-Woman Martha!
Ah, soul sister,
You did not cast yourself
at the feet of Jesus,
You stood before him,
questioning and challenging,
demanding more
than he had yet given.
For you were a woman
who always went to the edges—
peering at the possibilities,
passionate urger of new life,
pusher of boundaries,
role breaker.
Speaker of the truth—
you said it like it was,
and, in so doing,
you precipitated
the greatest miracle of them all.
Such disturbing and expectant faith eclipses
any inferior role of womanhood,
but stands up straight and shining,
proud and passionate,
prepared to change the world
from the kitchen.
Ah, Martha—Blessed Apostle,
Home-maker and Care-giver—
Woman for our times,
You have shown us the way.

Your solid, proud stance
comforts your sisters
baking still in soup kitchens,
homes, hospitals, schools,
and nursing homes throughout the world.
Your faithfulness
and dogged pursuit of life,
challenges us, soul sister,
to claim and honor
our own call to wholeness,
through service and compassion.
Ah, Martha, you confront us
with the task
of sacralizing our call,
with making holy our work
of home-making
and mothering.
Your voice awakens us
from complacency and submission
to claim the dignity of baking our bread
for the hungry of the world.
Your voice urges us
to claim the right
to bless and break our bread
and offer to all
who come to our table, saying:
Take this,
All of you
and eat it,
This is My Body,
Soul Sister.

The Infirm Woman

There was a woman there who for eighteen years had been possessed by a spirit which drained her strength. She was badly stooped—quite incapable of standing erect. When Jesus saw her, he called her to him and said, "Woman, you are free of your infirmity." He laid his hand on her, and immediately she stood up straight and began thanking God.

Luke 13:11-13

Infirm.
I guess that means
you couldn't do very much—
probably nothing at all.
Inactivity had left you flabby,
loose of flesh—
lacking firmness or solidity,

limbs all twisted and stiff.
So you must have
just shuffled along,
all bent down
like a crab.
You never saw the sky, then,
or myriad wondrous stars.
You never looked evenly
into the eyes of another,
but encountered only
the brush of their bodies
hurrying past you,
pre-occupied with the business
of the healthy,
leaving you behind,
(always behind),
trailing insignificance.
Your world, sister,
was largely the swirling sand
that rose from the slow shuffling
of your rough sandaled feet,
leaving you gray and dusty
as it made its home
in your dragging skirts.
People hardly notice you
creeping by—
they rarely do pay attention
to the disabled—
but avert their eyes,

somehow embarrassed
by the spectacle of disfigurement.
Does such a sight
perhaps remind us
of how vulnerable we all are
to the ravages of age or illness?
Are you our Shadow,
terrifying us
as you scuttle along, anonymously,
at the edges of our lives?
Ah, little lady,
will you, like so many
marked by physical disability,
be a continual affront
to our false dignity,
a distraction from our own
infirmity of spirit?
Will you be to us,
so self-assured of healthy body,
a person to be spurned and rejected,
doubly disabled
by our prejudice and fears?
For we rarely open our hearts
to people like you, sister.
Nor have we crafted our world
to accommodate your bent form.
So you must creep around our perimeters,
seeking access,
a way into our spaces.

You must double-check
entrances, exits, stairs and heights
to see if they welcome you
or leave you standing helpless,
like an infant
before a rising cliff.
Will we slip past you,
embarrassed?
Or will we see in you
a graced opportunity
to stretch our own crippled spirits,
recognizing
your inherent dignity,
and respecting the courage
of your endless silent struggle
to be part of a world
not fashioned for your infirmity?
Will we,
blessed with healthy bodies,
heal and soothe yours
simply by honoring
your whole bent self?
Will you become whole
by how we perceive you?
And will we,
loving like Jesus,
then become whole too?
Ah, Infirm Woman,
received and healed by Jesus,

stretch our souls—
shrunk small by insecurity.
Challenge us
to a deeper vision
that sees beneath the broken,
and celebrates
the unique wonder
of every human spirit.
Light up our shadows, sister,
and make us honest,
make us whole,
like you—
Soul Sister.

ℐhe Samaritan Woman

The hour was about noon. When a Samaritan woman came to draw water, Jesus said to her, "Give me a drink . . ." The Samaritan woman said to him, "You are a Jew. How can you ask me, a Samaritan and a woman, for a drink?" (Recall that Jews have nothing to do with Samaritans.) Jesus replied: "If only you recognized God's gift, and who it is that is asking you for a drink, you would have asked him instead, and he would have given you living water."

John 4:6-10

I waited for all the other women
to return from the well—
chattering and laughing,
carelessly spilling drops of their precious
     water

as they balanced their jugs
on sloping shoulders.
They walked together—
they always do—
clustering around a story,
a bit of news,
some whispered gossip,
about me, perhaps.
Yes—most probably about me.
But I would not show them
that I cared.
They would never know
how I held back my tears
and clenched my pain
tight close in my belly.
They never spoke to me—
these other women of my village
only shot me swift, scornful glances
as they passed my door.
Unlike their menfolk,
they despised my firm and slender body
and flinched from my dark beauty.
But still their menfolk
came to me,
sly and creeping in the night,
groping for love.
Everyone knew, of course.
I knew too,
that I would never be able to live

any other way.
After the first one—
so many years ago,
unwelcomed and violent—
it did not matter how many more
slipped through my door
in the night.
So now I live
as a leper to my sisters,
and I must walk alone—
excluded
from woman's most important ritual
of journeying to the well,
twice a day,
for water.
Early in the morning,
as the sun erupts in brilliant orange
against the hills,
they meet at the village edge
with whispered greetings,
nods and smiles.
Veils flapping
in the cool of early dawn,
they leave the village together
chattering and twittering
like a flock of birds.
They become but a cloud
hovering on the horizon.
I watch, aching with bitterness.

I hate the cloud.
Again at sunset,
the day's heat cooled,
and jugs long emptied,
they set out,
sharing stories and laughing,
sometimes weeping and consoling.
For this is woman-time—
our only time
to do what women like to do—
meet, listen, share,
men and children left behind—
excluded also
from sacred feminine ritual.
Fetching water is our time.
But not mine.
I must go alone at noon—
in the heat of the day—
when I can be sure
no one else will meet me,
and be shamed to look on me.
When the village eats and rests
behind closed doors,
I open mine,
and, furtive like my clients,
I slip into the light alone.
Balancing my jug,
I move swiftly
not daring a slow or leisured pace—

like the others.
I must hurry.
Hurry.
Elude their scorn . . .
Close to the well I stop,
scarce believing what I see—
a man resting there
in woman's sacred space.
I cannot hide,
nor return with empty jug.
But I know
I will be condemned
by this very encounter . . .
They will never believe
it was not planned.
But I must hurry—
quickly draw my water
with veiled eyes and practiced smile
belying my fear—
yet knowing he must shun me.
I must not speak.
It is not my place.
I have sinned enough.
I did not ask for this.
But it is not I
who breaks the rules—
the man, a Jew,
dares to speak to me!
Does he not know the law?

(It is not permitted for a Jew
to address a Samaritan—
for we are untouchables.)
Does he not know?
Yet softly, he speaks to me:
"Water,
give me water."
He—man, and Jew—
asking me for water!
I can scarce hide my shock.
He must be mad, of course.
But he is gentle . . .
He does not know me . . .
Ah, but no one has ever looked upon me
so tenderly!
I must tell him—
It is not done,
It is not right
that he should speak to me . . .
But he does.
He begins to tell me
strange things
about Living Water . . .
He must be mad!
Yet there is something about him
so peaceful and gentle . . .
(Am I the one who's mad?)
I must call his bluff.
He has no bucket—

how can he give water . . .
But still he talks—
offering flowing water,
the man says,
of a different kind—
welling up within—
an eternal spring
that would never dry up.
I am on the edge—
precipitous—
balancing my weight
before the dream of flowing water
that would never end . . .
Ah, I am so thirsty,
so deeply thirsty as I dare,
with mystic smile,
to imagine cleansing, freeing water
pouring over me . . .
Me?
Ah, Give it to me!
I cry aloud,
from my deep dark place of longing.
Fetch your husband,
says the man.
Ah, now, I am undone . . .
Bereft of the mirage of flowing water,
for husbands I have none,
I am that scorned
Woman Alone—

except in the darkness of the night.
And this man
does not know me.
He cannot know me . . .
But, ah, he does—
for he tells me all,
reminds me of my story,
reveals my shame
in woman's sacred space.
I am doubly condemned.
But then, oh, wondrous moment!
He does not damn me
but blesses me—me,
the woman scorned!
He tells me who he is—
the Christ—
the one we all await,
the one who is to come, is here!
Now!
With me!
Talking with me
in sacred space . . .
I am swelling with a joy and freedom
I have never known!
There is a rush like cleansing water
running through me,
leaving me light as air.
I have no need now
for my jar of clay.

I run

with the Living Water!

I run with the Good News entrusted to me—

to me—

by the Christ

who waited for me,

received and filled me at the well

where women gather.

I am no longer afraid and shamed.

I am your soul sister.

Honored, blessed,

bearer of new life,

First witness of the Christ

amongst us

Who broke the rules of exclusion,

Who dared to speak to a woman,

Who asked a favor from such as I,

then chose me

the rejected one,

chose me

the sinner,

chose me

the woman

to run, oh, so filled up,

with such Good News.

The Woman Caught in Adultery

The scribes and the Pharisees led a woman forward who had been caught in adultery. They made her stand there in front of everyone . . . "Teacher," they said to him, "this woman has been caught in the act of adultery. In the law, Moses ordered such women to be stoned. What do you say about the case?" . . . When they persisted in their questioning, he straightened up and said to them, "Let the man among you who has no sin be the first to cast a stone at her." . . . Then the audience drifted away one by one . . . This left him alone with the woman . . . and he said to her, "Woman, where did they disappear to? Has no one condemned you?" "No one sir," she answered. Jesus said, "Nor do I condemn you. You may go. But from now on, avoid sin."

John 8:2-11

I remember the sound of stones
cracking on the sidewalk
as we fled into the night,
pursued by Outrage.
Outrage
flung the sharp hard things
at our retreating shadows.
Screams of abuse—
carried further than the stones—
went before us
proclaiming our shame
to all the world.
In that time and place—
walking with the broken-hearted—
I had been mistaken
for a prostitute,
seller of sex,
lover of all men,
seducer,
object of disdain and scorn.
Fear tightened my heart
as feet pounded away
from bright lights
and Outrage
to crouch in an alley,
anonymous and unseen,

in the shadows of the night.
How I trembled there,
gasping for air
to steady
the thudding of my heart.
Outrage
had not left me intact;
my soul was forever seared
with the memory
of shame unwarranted
and the terrible humiliation
of stones—
cold, hard,
aimed to bruise and break
my own soft body.
I have never forgotten
the stoning.
I have never forgotten
the hatred
that pursued me,
longing to inflict
its righteous pain.
I have never forgotten
the tensing of all muscles
expectant of the thud of stone
against my yielding skin.
Oh, I have never forgotten
the public shaming!
But now I am no longer

pursued.
I am only observer
of another's story—
a woman caught in adultery
they say—
Accused of breaking
the Moral Code—
though there is no sign
of co-conspirator or partner.
She stands alone now,
no time no place to flee,
but cornered
by her male accusers—
Outrage,
stuttering its condemnation,
itching to lift the stones
lying waiting on the ground.
No questions here, either,
just the certainty of guilt
and a palpable longing
to punish and annihilate.
Here is the woman
who broke the law of Moses,
Here is the woman
who broke the law of man,
Here is the woman
who broke the law of the Taliban.
Here is the woman
who broke the law of the church,

Here is the woman
who broke the law of patriarchy,
Here is the woman
    the woman
    the woman,
who broke the law
    the law
    the law,
designed by Outrage
to condemn
all forms of passion
and woman love.
Here she is—
caught loving
caught holding
caught in tenderness—
caught in woman sin.
There are many names for you,
they echo down the ages—
sharp and scarlet like the apple
Eve gave to Adam.
Your names still ring,
loud and clear,
down our city streets,
I heard them—
tart, whore, tramp!
Woman caught in sin!
Dragged from male partner
and left to stand alone—

shamed—
in the market place.
I see the proud toss of your head,
belying your terror
as your beads and bracelets flash
like the fire in your eyes.
But I also know
the damp sweat of fear
prickling through your clothing,
now clutched
tightly around you
in useless protection.
I have seen you so many times,
standing beneath
our city lights,
strutting in the brothel,
awaiting the lust and rape—
knowing nothing else,
not knowing, either,
whether you are
to be loved or beaten,
caressed or killed.
So you must stand
proud and brave
in your cruel reality
ready for anything,
fearing everything.
Your look is colder
than the stones

you know they itch
to throw.
They must not discover
the torrents of tears
damned up behind
those glittering eyes.
They must not find out
how broken up and afraid you are
beneath your shining beads.
But there is one who knows.
There is one
who sees so deeply—
compassion burning—
that all the stones melt
before his gaze.
Through all the pride and vanity,
all the posturing
and the primping,
through all the anger
and the bitterness,
the pain and despair,
He sees the God in you—
claiming you
ever precious and beloved—
though you're yet unaware
of your dignity
and the river of grace
which runs through you.
It is before this man,

whose eyes are tender,
that you are brought to stand
awaiting judgment.
Your accusers gather round,
fingering chosen stones,
awaiting approval
of their righteousness
and your guilt.
But Jesus does not speak.
His silence
condemns no one.
It hangs
in the still warm air
forcing eyes inward,
turning certainty
into confusion.
The words are gently spoken:
Let the one without sin
throw the first stone.
Truth searing!
Words ripping open respectability
to reveal maggoty hypocrisy
in hiding,
leaving sin trailing
like a tattered tail
behind each one of us—
shadows clinging defiantly
beneath the coats of righteousness.
Slowly, reluctantly,

fingers are loosened,
and one by one,
stones are dropped—not thrown.
And one by one,
the accusers—
eyes cast down
like their stones—
turn away
in acknowledgment
of the Word,
the Truth,
the Light
that shone upon their shadows.
The woman is free,
released and made whole
by compassion
more powerful and brighter
than the accumulated darkness
of all humanity's sin.
She is now
more honest and true
than she has ever been,
And we—
soul sister, soul brother—
must also be set free,
to recognize in ourselves
the sharp and broken
bits of stone
we carry,

acknowledging shadows dug deep
in our souls
and daring to lay them bare
before the light
of grace
that ever hovers—
daring us to integrity.
It is we
who must break the chains,
loose the bonds
and dispel the shame
which cowers and cripples
those condemned by righteousness.

Soul sister!
Woman freed by grace—
soften our eyes,
melt our hearts,
and loosen from our fingers
the stones we have gathered
and stored in our souls.

In the sun of a late summer
the women gathered
to tell their stories—
so like yours, soul sister!
They remembered
with awful sadness,
what once they had been

and all their given labels—
street walkers, drug addicts, hookers—
the fallen and the failures of society.
But no longer.
From fall to fall
they had journeyed,
until one day
they stood up straight,
having heard
for the first time
words of compassion,
having seen
for the first time
(broken open by grace)
a light screaming for freedom
in the deeps of their souls.
And they sobbed
for the brightness of the light
and the warmth of its presence.
For years then,
never forgetting that glimpse
of great mercy,
they stumbled on—
pursuing the newborn thing
which whispered
a lifetime's forgiveness
and brought them,
still standing,
to that late summer day

where they gathered, still awed,
by new life.
Now teachers, counselors
and healers,
singers of new songs,
they collected stones
from the soft beach—
hard, solid and shining wet . . .
And I remembered
the stones
sharp, hard things
that once had been flung
by Outrage.
Stones now stroked with delight,
gathered as gifts—
Comfort stones
Serenity stones—
by the women once caught
in adultery.
These stones,
one woman breathed,
eyes shining,
will be for our sisters,
to hold tight close
in times of stress
and times of fear.
We will transform these stones—
bless them,

and make them new—
like us!

And so we did.
Standing in sacred circle
of prayer and grace
we passed our stones
from sister to sister,
breathing on them blessing,
washing them in tears,
transforming stones into treasures—
no longer missiles of hate—
but objects of solace and comfort
soaked in blessing,
symbols of compassion,
to be passed on
from soul sister to soul sister.
Neither, sister,
Oh, neither do we—condemn you.

The Woman with the Hemorrhage

A woman had been afflicted with a hemorrhage for a dozen years . . . She had heard about Jesus and came up behind him in the crowd and put her hand to his cloak. "If I just touch his clothing," she thought, "I shall get well." Immediately her flow of blood dried up . . . Wheeling about in the crowd, he began to ask, "Who touched my clothing?" . . . Fearful and beginning to tremble now . . . she fell in front of him and told him the whole truth. He said to her, "Daughter, it is your faith that has cured you . . ."

Mark 5:25-34

You are crouched low, my sister,
swathed in black
to hide your woman body.
I wince

before your desperation.
The hollowness of your eyes
reveals only your curled up self
bent beneath
your shame and humiliation.
But ah,
how could you stand, sister,
weighted down
by the condemnation of your world?
Your condition
damned by all.
Your unceasing flow of woman blood
was a curse they said
(Not symbol of fertility)
demanding isolation—
like AIDS.
In your eternal quarantine
none could hold you,
none could touch you.
All were shamed
to look on you, sister.
Cursed you were—
crouching like a cur
in your corner,
yearning for the deliverance of death—
so long in coming.
Twelve years—
a lifetime it seemed—
of isolation and loneliness

No meds.
No insurance.
No cure.
No hope.
What were your thoughts, sister,
through all those silent days and nights?
Or were you too afraid
to think?
Too damned to dream
in your all-pervading darkness?
Did you simply
weep away
all your tears
till even your soul
dried up?
Did you feel your spirit
slowly suffocate
beneath the blanket of rejection
that weighed on you?
You have sisters, here,
soul friend.
Women hidden way
beneath harsh cultures
of female oppression;
crouching also
in dark corners,
bodies swathed in veils
to hide their beauty
and the tears in their eyes.

Your sisters are imprisoned still,
forbidden to walk in the light,
afraid to stand up tall,
deprived of education and employment,
starved of light and loveliness.
We glimpse them now and then
on television—
dark shadows
furtively fleeing from camera lights,
angled to capture
their blindness.
We read about their horrific despair
in the newspapers.
You would recognize them, sister.
For you know their story.
And yours reaches out
across the centuries to touch them
as no other could
but the one that shares
their hell.
What do you tell them,
across the ages, sister?
Whisper to me, sister,
what was it
that happened to you?
When did life stir in you again?
Was it a voice you heard or
a dream you dreamt?
What drove you—risking death—

from your tomb, sister?
Was it a little seed
that burst in you,
pulsing in defiance—
then madness?
What happened
to raise you up straight
no longer curled in your corner?
Tell me, sister, tell me—
that I might whisper your story
and your secret
to your sisters imprisoned
across the globe!

One warm sweet day
listening to life
moving beyond my walls,
I suddenly heard
mysteries breathed
that set my heart
fast beating hard—
I heard
of the blind seeing
and the deaf hearing
and the dumb speaking.
Ridiculous, wondrous things!
And I, who was dead,
knew there could be no life
in dead things.

Already wrapped tightly in my grave,
I dismissed
the wild claims
of the whisperers,
and clutched tightly
to my dying—
fiercely denying dreams and miracles.
But, ah,
the little bit of light, audacious,
that had pierced my darkness,
held fast in my deeps
and would not
be extinguished.
Dallying and dancing
in my guts
like a newborn thing leaping
for the light,
it thrust me from my knees,
quickening my long-numbed muscles
with strange new life
that raised me up—
all trembling.
Erect and fearful
I stood terrified
on my threshold.
And then, it seemed to me,
that it was better to die
for life
than die from despair.

So, gathering my skirts around me,
I pushed open
my long shut door
and, all tingling with terror,
stepped from my cell
on warm and sandy soil.
Alert now, for the first time
since I was a girl running free,
I sought the light
which shone in me,
I pursued the whispers
which beckoned me,
further and further
from my dungeoned self
towards wide open spaces.
All the while
fear still held my heart,
screeching retreat,
and doubts rose up
to shadow my light—too late!
For I had already seen it,
pure and free
in my mind's eye.
And, oh, it delighted me so—
I would die for it!
So, step by step,
faltering—near falling—
but persistent,
I kept on coming

towards that space—transparent.
I knew I need only
reach out and touch—
dare break death's rule . . .
Stretch further than I'd ever known
to share my secret dreams
and tell my story—
speak aloud my unheard truth,
scream my dying
in the face of life.
And I did . . .
From, ah, so deep a place,
my sorrow and anguish tumbled out
before the sunlight
which, gathering up my grief,
absorbed it,
leaving me
resurrected,
Alive!
And in that wild, free moment,
the blind could see,
the deaf could hear,
the dumb could speak,
as now I do for you.
Ah, sisters,
how loud and clear rang my voice
that day!
How I ran, delirious,
across the open plains,

singing my song of life!
Listen, sisters,
I sing it still—
Listen deeply
in the darkness that envelops you,
absorb the secrets
that gestate in silence—
germinating life yet too tender
for blazing light,
whisper your dreams
in prison cell,
nourish the grace
of your Self
in broken moments,
and you will hear
in your own expectant breathing,
the first notes—so soft—
of my song,
rising, rising,
clear and sweet—
for you,
Soul Sister.

The Daughter of Jairus

Seeing Jesus, [Jairus] fell at his feet and made this earnest appeal: "My little daughter is critically ill. Please come and lay your hands on her so that she may get well and live." . . . He had not finished speaking when people from the official's house arrived saying, "Your daughter is dead . . ." Jesus disregarded the report . . . and said to the official, "Fear is useless. What you need is trust." . . . Jesus took the child's father and mother . . . where the child lay. Taking her hand he said to her, "Talitha, koum," which means, "Little girl get up." The girl, a child of twelve, stood up immediately and began to walk around.

Mark 5:22-24, 35-43

Daughter—daughter of Jairus!
We do not know your name—

only that of your father
whose love for you
drove him to his knees
before the gathered crowd.
In a patriarchal culture where men
stood aloof and proud,
your father, a wealthy CEO—
accustomed to giving orders
and being in full control—
fell and wept
before a homeless carpenter.
Oblivious of his humiliation
and the pity and wonder
of staring eyes,
he broke down in public,
for you—
whose name we do not know.
But, ah, we know your father,
who cared for you more than all
his dignity and reputation,
and to whom your life,
though small,
was precious.
He held your slender girl body
in a place of honor and pride—
above his own.
That, indeed, is how it should be
for the weakest and the smallest.
We are all potential parents—

gifted with the instinct
to care for and protect
the little ones
of any nation, tribe or color.
Have we forgotten?
Have we disempowered ourselves,
burying in disbelief
that salvific grace
that would render us passionate prophets,
co-creators with the Holy One,
intent on healing
broken hearts and bodies?
Such a love,
indignant for life,
was deep in your father,
daughter of Jairus.
For he risked ridicule
to save you.
In a culture where girl children
were ranked beneath donkeys,
your father treasured you!
He dared cry
before a wandering peasant, believing
(amazing ridiculous faith)
that he carried within him
(as do we all)
the transformative power of God.
The miracle was surely
as much in your father

as in Jesus
who was moved and struck
by such blind and naked faith.
It is the kind of faith
which leaves respectability and convention
curled up
like a small irrelevant ball
in the face of mystery.
It is a faith
for which we deeply hunger,
yet shun.
For it requires a fall
into the grace of God within us—
and we are afraid to fall.
Nor do we, unlike Jairus,
weep and cry in public,
allowing ourselves to acknowledge
how broken up we are—
and daring to reach
for deep healing.
In our determined got-togetherness
we become unconscious
of the power of God's seed
that would swell in our souls,
daring us to miracles,
and inciting us
to be about the business of resurrection
for which the whole world
longs and waits

staring at us
from TV screens,
wide eyes glazing
in the dust of Iraq.
And there they are again—
the children of Sudan and Mexico,
Nicaragua, India
and Mozambique—
the children of the world,
waiting for our miracles
and wasting right in front of us!
And what is it that afflicts
our own—
driving us to demand Ritalin, Clonodine
and Welbutrin
and all manner of pills and potions
to still their deep disturbances?
What must we do
before the pernicious diseases—
child cancer, leukemia,
despair and anxiety—
that cripple our own children,
leaving them limp and silent?
Ah, we need you, Jairus!
We need the passion that burned in you
for the health and life of your little one.
We need the desperate determination
which sent you running and humbled
to the feet of Jesus

begging for new life!
We need the kind of unselfish love
that will topple us from high places
of righteousness and political strategies,
of retaliation and sanctions
and lead us, instead,
to look with compassion
into the eyes of children in pain
who know nothing of sanctions—
but only of the hurt
and the ache in their bellies.
It is the children who must drive us,
like you, Jairus,
into public places,
weeping for mercy and
stretching out for healing.
Miracles will come about only
when we fall from arrogance and power
to a place of deep conversion.
It is our tears, then,
which will bring about
the healing of our world.
And maybe then,
when we come to honor and love
all the little ones,
putting them first and before all else,
our lives will shine, splendid and pure,
in the light of God—
as brilliant as that

which must have shone
in your father's eyes,
daughter of Jairus,
when you were raised from death.
Ah, child of Jairus!
You are forever now,
a testimony to a father's love,
and a driven, shining faith
which is all that is required
to raise us up—
Like you, Soul Sister.

The Penitent Woman

There was a certain Pharisee who invited Jesus to dine with him. Jesus went to the Pharisee's home and reclined to eat. A woman known in the town to be a sinner learned that he was dining in the Pharisee's home. She brought a vase of perfumed oil and stood behind him at his feet, weeping so that her tears fell upon his feet. Then she wiped them with her hair, kissing them and perfuming them with the oil.

Luke 7:36-38

I think you have been weeping,
my sister,
for your eyes, limpid,
shine moist and haunted
and I see in them
a grief locked tight and hiding

beneath the glitter of favors
hanging from your hair.
What is your story, sister?
Where have you been?
What did you do
to carry such pain in your eyes—
heavier, indeed,
than the coins flashing
upon your brow?
No name for you but sinner—
shrouded in public shame,
breaker of the moral code.
You are anonymous—
but for sin.
Did you sell yourself
for the coins that hang upon you?
We will never know why . . .
But we do know, sister,
that there is always a reason
for despair.
We do know, sister,
that women like you
are not born intent on sin
and self-destruction,
but come,
like all of us,
full of expectations that our lives
will be happy and fruitful.

We women have come to understand
that selling ourselves
is not something we desire
and dream of,
but is, rather,
an act of self-annihilation
driven by despair.
We know that beneath it all
there is an untold story
locked in childhood memory—
too horrific for the light of day.
We know this, sister,
because so many others
have walked your path
of condemnation—
and even come to tell it.
The violence done to woman
is no longer a secret.
Now we see
beneath the baubles,
now we see
beneath the masks
and we call you sister—
not sinner.
You have your own brave story.
Risking the anger and the ridicule
of those around you,
cloaked in their shallow respectability,

you broke through
their righteous ranks,
slipping your silken veils
past their long stiff robes,
gate-crashing the patriarchal party,
bearing, tight to your bosom,
your rich and precious perfume.
They did not know
who you were, sister—
only what you had done.
It was enough
to leave them aghast
at your intrusion and your daring.
But you were driven
by something far deeper
than they would ever know or feel—
a passion
that poured right out
from your belly
and flowed into warm tears
that fell upon the feet of Jesus.
Your tears were your story, sister,
told for the first time
to the man who looked upon you
with compassion—
illuminating your soul, sister,
and revealing all the longing
breaking from within it.

With eyes that penetrated
he knew, sister,
who you were.
And he loved you
for yourself.
Not so,
the crowd of accusers
who gathered around,
in shock and disgust
at the spectacle of raw emotion,
right before their eyes.
How could anyone
(their looks betrayed)
with a modicum of honor
receive a woman such as you!
The lovely smell of your perfume
rose from the feet of Jesus,
assailing with floral bouquet
the outraged dignity
of the dinner guests.
Disapproving,
brows furrowed,
they mumbled about the poor
and the wanton, inappropriate waste
of expensive oil
poured on the body of Jesus.
(They did not know who he was either.)
But Jesus knew,

and you knew, sister,
that the perfume
bathing you in sweetness—
like clouds of grace—
belonged to you both.
So you knelt,
expectant of compassion,
at the feet of the one
who knew you and loved you
for yourself
and for your inner truth.
Like the perfume you unstopped,
it was for you, sister,
a moment of release
as all the crushed
and wrapped up pain within you
dissolved,
all the insults and blows of the years
you had borne,
faded now—
dispelling all despair forever
in a moment of grace and honesty.
Now, sister, you are free—
your story told,
your love revealed
to all of us.
Our invitation is to look deeper
than we do,

to intuit and honor
what so often lies
beneath a surface
of denial, anger and diminishment,
grace pulsing to break through.
I once knew
another woman like you.
She ran a brothel in the city,
managing sex
for her clients and her girls.
The money she surreptitiously slipped
into her roomy pockets
was exchanged for sexual acts—
considered still
one of the greatest sins of all.
Even so,
she welcomed me into her home
and place of business,
plying me with cookies, tea
and homemade cake.
The clients,
smart, professional men
in politics and business,
(taking a quick break for sex
from their offices downtown),
slipped furtively in and out
the darkened rooms
like thieves—

eyes down but wary.
When all was still,
after the lunch-time rush,
the madam thrust a twenty-dollar bill
down my blouse, muttering:
"For your ministry."
I was horrified
knowing that the money
had come from prostitution.
My whole self protested . . .
Until I saw
the tears and longing in her eyes
crying out unspoken plea:
Do not reject me too . . .
Then I remembered you, sister,
and your story.
Her twenty-dollar bill
became a waft of perfumed oil
moving in her sad, dark home
like a whispered breath of sweetness
playing on my senses.
Who was I to judge
the heart which broke
into that moment,
spilling kindness and longing?
Who was I to dismiss
her story
because I did not know it?

No matter, sisters,
we are all capable,
in the midst of murky deeds,
of bearing perfume,
and shedding hot repentant tears
to wash and bless each other—
as you did, Soul Sister.

Mary Magdalene

Meanwhile, Mary [Magdalene] stood weeping beside the tomb. Even as she wept, she stooped to peer inside, and there she saw two angels in dazzling robes . . . "Woman," they asked her, "why are you weeping?" She answered them, "Because the Lord has been taken away . . ." She turned around and caught sight of Jesus standing there. But she did not know him . . . Jesus said to her, "Mary!" She turned to him and said [in Hebrew], "Rabbouni!" (meaning "Teacher").

John 20:11-16

Ah, Mary of Magdala,
they did not tell us
your story.
It was lost,
buried deep

in layers
of fear and denial,
that such a one as you—
Female,
fiercely loyal friend of Jesus—
could walk so closely
with the Son of God,
never leaving his side
even as you stood
before the gates of hell.
What sickness wracked
your woman body, Mary,
before the one you came to love
raised you into fullness,
dispelling all
that beat you down?
Did you creep around
the dusty streets of Galilee
wracked by cancerous cells?
Or did some unknown virus
sap your spirit—
leaving you
wrung out and desolate.
What dread sickness was it, Mary,
that gripped you
with all of seven symptoms?
They did not tell us
your story . . .
But we know

your spirit was battered
in a society
which had no place for you.
Was your sickness then
a soul-sickness, sister?
Were the demons
that devoured you,
offsprings of despair
in a patriarchal culture
where your voice
could never be spoken,
your words
never heard?
Could it be, sister,
that, beaten down,
into silence and submission,
your would-be powerful spirit
shriveled into sickness,
bitter in your belly?
Did you fear
the very intelligence
that warned you to be mute
lest your woman voice—
disallowed in public—
break out in mighty scream
provoking rage and retaliation
from the ones
who made the rules?
Or could it be

that your very talents—
marking you a misfit—
drove you
to self-doubt and shame,
rejection of your very self?
They did not tell us, Mary.
They did not tell us your story.
Could your seven demons
be those very ones
that reside still in your sisters,
two thousand years later,
cowering in shadowy apartments,
brutalized by
domestic violence
and believing it deserved?
Afraid to speak,
to break the chains
that bind them.
Were you, Mary,
as spirit-dead as they?
Did fear and silence
drive you
to the sickness
of the dying?
And are you still alive
with us,
Mary of Magdala,
in those women in North Africa who,
forced to spend their lives

in the confines of their huts,
are driven
to induce abortions
to gain hospital entrance?
There they will meet,
in pain-filled conspiracy,
their sisters
and hold hands and conversation
to hold back,
for a while,
incipient madness
ever looming before them
through the silence and solitude
of their untold story.
Or are you
our sisters in prison, Mary?
Locked up
because they could not say no
to the crack cocaine
that dulled the violence
of their lives,
misting over memories
of multiple rapes?
Ah, Mary of Magdala,
were you also imprisoned
by your story
never told?
Until one day,
Ah, one glorious, glorious day,

destined to shine
through history,
beckoning
like a flaming beacon
to women throughout the ages,
He looked upon you, Mary,
and saw
your soul beauty
starved for light
and voice.
The man, Jesus,
capable like a lightning rod
of burning through darkness,
recognized you,
Mary of Magdala,
as his own—
friend, companion, apostle.
It was in that moment
of recognition,
of claiming and honoring
all you were,
that Jesus dispelled in you
the demons of fear, doubt
and repression, raising you up
into fullness,
calling forth
your powerful presence—
long fetal-curled in womb.
Ah, Mary of Magdala,

you knew first
your own rising from the dead!
How radiant you shone!
Your joy leaping up unfettered
as your dreams spilled out
in the free hot breeze
of a village in Galilee!
How was it with you, then,
as freedom led you dancing
in the market place?
By his side now
strong you stood,
supportive and affirming
of the One
who broke your chains.
You never left him, Mary,
faithful friend,
even as the authorities closed in—
horrified at freedom,
trembling with anger
before equality's brave stance.
But never again, Mary,
in spite of the threats,
would you be less
than you knew yourself to be.
Were you afraid, Mary,
as you aligned yourself
with Jesus—
the one who set you free?

Did your woman heart beat faster
as the crowds grew bigger
and his words spread
through the land?
Did you nurture
a fragile hope
that the crowds
would be raised up too
and throw off
their demons of oppression?
You knew, Mary,
what that would mean,
you knew that life
would never, ever,
be the same again.
You knew, Mary,
that that was dangerous.
Resistance always is.
But you stayed with him.
You listened more deeply
to the words he spoke
and they took root
in you—
strengthening, affirming, guiding.
And so you stood firm
against the whisperings,
the threats, the rumors.
You held his hand—
as women do the ones

they love.
You prepared food for him—
as women do for hungry ones.
You supported him—
as women do for those in need.
But, above all,
you loved the man, Jesus,
and he you,
Mary of Magdala.
So when they came for him,
you went too,
waiting and fretting
outside the prison walls
as women do
when their menfolk are inside.
No one can measure
the anguish that washed
through you—
for no one told your story.
But others have lived it, Mary,
the mothers and wives,
the daughters and sisters
of El Salvador and Colombia,
Russia and Iraq,
Sudan and Bosnia,
Guatemala and South Africa,
and many, many more.
Women who waited,
and still wait, for news of their men

taken in the night
by soldiers, bombs, bullets
and the Authorities—
so afraid of freedom.
Your sisters, Mary,
keep their vigil yet,
as you kept yours.
. . . Until the verdict was announced,
and you knew,
with a sickening fall of heart,
that it was all over.
The one who raised you up,
the one you came to love,
was also to be raised,
agonizingly,
in front of you
and before all the crowd
who heard his words
but never understood them
as you did.
You could have fled the agony
of watching
the killing.
The world would have understood—
even encouraged you
to spare yourself the suffering . . .
But you followed him
Mary of Magdala,
right to the end

and the place of execution.
Love does that sort of thing.
You led the women
even as your spirit was hurled
into the depths of hell
and the men fled the pain
in fear of apprehension.
You were there, Mary,
walking all the way
and watching him—
all bloodied—
stumble and fall three times.
How could you endure, Mary?
But you did.
You watched them fell and nail
the man who raised you up.
Slowly his life ebbed away
before your eyes.
Ah, Mary,
something in you too,
must have died that day!
Then followed the waiting,
the long grievous waiting
for the funeral rites—
the washing and anointing of the body.
In the early light
of Sabbath
you gathered with the women
and hurried to the place

where they had laid him,
clutching your ointments
and your perfumed oils
to lavish on the one
you loved.
Claiming,
as women throughout history
have claimed,
the last service of love—
to stroke and kiss
their dead.
But your dead was gone—
black space staring
where they had left him.
Deepening your own black space—
leaving you naked in grief . . .
Not even the comfort of a body
for you to bathe with whisperings.
Ah, Mary!
You knew well
the desperation
of those mothers and wives,
sisters and daughters
who watch the hearse
pull out from dark prison walls
carrying the remains
of their executed loved ones
off into a grey dawn.
Where have they taken him?

Your story of the
empty grave
was dismissed as rambling—
distraught woman-nonsense.
But you returned
to the empty space

ed there—
leave the ground
cious
ush of his skin.
re,
ep and empty space,
ispered
, Mary,
into another world—

lm of God—
miracle,
d,
of God

name—

nd chosen.
h you then,
la?
place of revelation,
singular woman witness

of the Resurrection?
How was it,
to be so bereft
and then be thrust, still weeping,
into the bliss
of the Realm of God?
To run then,
with that vision—
that news of life—
to those who lived in fear?
Ah, Mary,
we your sisters
need to hear your running
and your story
resurrected and dusted from the tomb
of scriptural exegesis
into the bright sunlight.
We need to claim
your vision
breaking through
dead history
into our warm lives.
We, the women in prison,
women waiting,
women silenced,
women battered,
women who weep alone by the grave
need to find you,
Mary of Magdala.

In the torn threads
of our own journeys,
we need to weave you, Mary,
sister and friend,
into our lives
that we might
stir and rise,
fluttering in the hope
of new beginnings,
no matter how long dead
we have lain
in the ground.
Ah, then, Mary,
brave woman of Magdala,
we too will run
from our tombs
singing our song
of resurrection
with you, soul sister,
into the bright,
bright sun.

Of Related Interest

Christ All Merciful
Megan McKenna
Icons by William Hart McNichols, S.J.

ISBN 1-57075-449-7, paperback, full color

The wondrous saving power of Jesus comes alive in both image and word. While 18 beautiful, glowing icons lead us to see God face to face, the accompanying reflections call us to become this image of God, to put on the new life of Christ.

The Bride
Images of the Church
Daniel Berrigan
Icons by William Hart McNichols

ISBN 1-57075-305-9, paperback, full color

Portrays in words and art the diverse face of the Church – the Bride of Christ. Twenty full-color icons include martyrs and saints, prisoners of conscience and theologians, women and men.
"A stunning, devastating, and uplifting prayer book for the 21st-century Christian."   *–Sojourners*

Mary, Mother of All Nations
Megan McKenna
Icons by William Hart McNichols, S.J.

ISBN 1-57075-325-3, paperback, full color

Beautiful reflections and prayers by the noted author and storyteller accompany 31 luminous icons of Mary, Mother of Jesus.

Please support your local bookstore, or call 1-800-258-5838.
For a free catalogue, please write us at
Orbis Books, Box 308
Maryknoll NY 10545-0308
Or visit our website and order online at www.maryknollmall.org

Thank you for reading *Soul Sisters*.
We hope you enjoyed it.